MAGNETS

AND HOW TO USE THEM

By TILLIE S. PINE and JOSEPH LEVINE
Illustrated by BERNICE MYERS

SCHOLASTIC INC.

New York Toronto London Auckland Sydney

You may also want to read these books by Tillie S. Pine and Joseph Levine:

ELECTRICITY AND HOW WE USE IT

SOUNDS ALL AROUND

THE INDIANS KNEW

AIR ALL AROUND

WATER ALL AROUND

ISBN: 0-590-02428-0

The original edition of MAGNETS AND HOW TO USE THEM, published by McGraw-Hill Book Co., Inc., was illustrated by Anne Marie Jauss.

23 22 21 20 19   7/8

To Mona and Susan
who always want to know
how **and** *why*

How do people use magnets in their work?

What things will stick to magnets?

Can a magnet work through things?

What part of the magnet is strongest?

Why do we make horseshoe magnets?

How can magnets be used to help you
find direction?

What is the right way to use a compass
that you buy in a store?

How can you make your own magnet?

How can you make
   an on-and-off magnet (electromagnet)?

How can an electromagnet pick up
   and drop a heavy load?

Where do electromagnets work in your home?

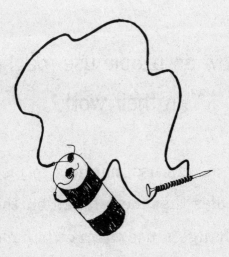

This book will show you how to find out.

How do people use magnets
in their work?

Dressmakers use magnets to pick up pins
and needles that have fallen on the floor.

Sign hangers use magnet hammers
to hold the tacks that are used to nail
up signs.

Magnets make work easier!

Teachers sometimes use magnet boards
in school. They can use them to teach words
and numbers to children.

Sometimes people use magnet boards
when they play word games on television.

What things will stick to magnets?

Touch a tack with the end of your magnet.
What happens?
The tack sticks to the magnet!

Now touch a nail and a paper clip,
and see if they stick to the magnet.

Touch a tooth-pick with the magnet.

Touch a dime.

Touch a rubber band.

What happens now?

They do not stick to the magnet.

Look around in your house and find

a pencil,

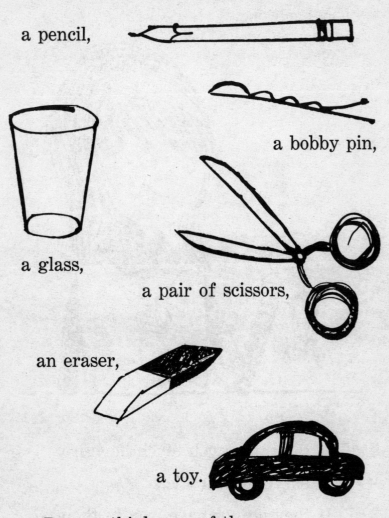

a bobby pin,

a glass,

a pair of scissors,

an eraser,

a toy.

Do you think any of these
will stick to your magnet?

Try each one.

If the things you touch have iron
in them, they will stick.

If they do not have iron in them,
they will not stick.

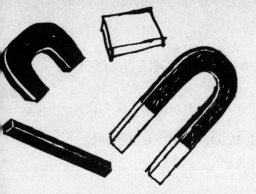

Long magnets
Short magnets
Fat magnets
Thin magnets

Boys and girls play with toys that
have magnets in them.

Some sailing toys, fishing games,
building toys, and trick toys
have magnets in them.

You can have fun playing with
games and toys that have magnets in them.

Can a magnet work through things?

Put a small piece of paper on a table.

Touch the paper with your magnet.

Does it stick?

Of course not!

Why not?

Paper has no iron in it.

Now place the paper over a paper clip.

Touch the paper right over the clip

with your magnet.

Lift!

Up they come — paper, clip, and all!

A magnet, you see, works through paper.

What do you think would happen if you used an open handkerchief instead of paper over the clip?

Exactly the same thing would happen.

A magnet also works through cloth.

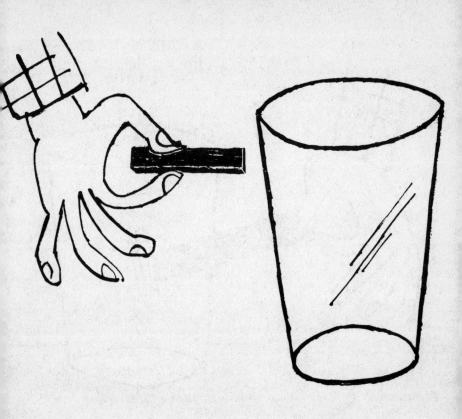

Now try this:

Touch a drinking glass with your magnet.

Why doesn't the glass stick to the magnet?

Glass has no iron in it.

Put a clip inside the glass.

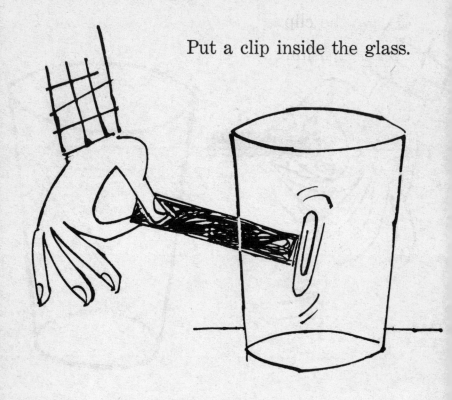

Touch the magnet to the outside of the glass near the clip.

Slide the magnet around the outside of the glass. Watch the clip. You will see it move around inside the glass.

A magnet, you see, works through glass.

Leave the clip in the glass and add water.

Now go fishing for the clip with the magnet.

Surprised?

The clip jumps at the magnet

as soon as the magnet gets close to it.

A magnet, you see, works through water.

Magnets make iron things
stick to them.

Magnets can work through
    paper
        cloth
            glass
                and water!

What part of the magnet is strongest?

You have been using only the ends
of the magnet.

Do you think the middle of the magnet
can pick up things that have iron in them,
just as the ends do?

Try it and see!

Cut up some steel wool.

Put the little bits of steel wool
on a table.

Lay the magnet on top of the steel wool.

What happens?

Can you believe what you see?

The steel wool is sticking only near the
ends of the magnet.

And —

there is almost no steel wool sticking to the
middle of the magnet.

Why not?

Only the ends of your magnet are strong enough to pick up the bits of steel wool.

Remember all the things in your house that you picked up with your magnet?

Now try to pick up these same things, using the middle of your magnet.

You will see that the middle
of your magnet is not strong enough
to pick up some of the heavier things.
There are some things
only the ends can pick up.

All magnets are strongest at their ends!

Straight magnets—

Curved magnets—

Both kinds have strong ends!

The ends of magnets are sometimes

far apart, like this:

We call this a bar magnet.

The ends of a magnet are sometimes
close together, like this:

Or like this:

Do you see why we call one
a horseshoe magnet and the other
a U magnet?

Bar magnets have strong ends far apart.

Horseshoe magnets and U magnets
have strong ends close together.

Why do we make horseshoe magnets and U magnets?

You can find out why we make
horseshoe magnets and U magnets:
Make believe *you* are a magnet.
Spread your arms.
You are a bar magnet.
Your hands are the ends.

Now pick up a chair with one of your
outstretched hands.
Hard, isn't it?

Now try it this way:

Put your hands close together in front of you.

You are a horseshoe magnet or a U magnet.

Your hands are the ends again.

Use both hands to pick up the chair.

See how easily it comes up!

You can lift things better
when you use both your hands.

A magnet, too, works better when
both ends are close together. Then they
can work together to pick up things
that have iron in them.

Straight magnets —

Curved magnets —

Both kinds have strong ends!

The ends can pick up things

that have iron in them.

But —

both ends working together can

pick up *heavier* things that have

iron in them.

When you are not using your magnet,

put an iron nail across each end of it.

This will keep your magnet strong for a long

time.

How can magnets be used
to help you find direction?

Which way is north? A magnet can show you.

Do you want to see how?

Tie one end of a thin string

around the middle of the magnet.

Walk to the middle of the room.

Hold the loose end of the string,

and let the magnet hang down.

Soon the magnet will stop turning.

Ask someone to tell you which side of the room is the north side.

One end of your magnet will point toward that side of the room.

Print the letter N on the end of the magnet pointing toward the north.

Now you can find "north" wherever you are.

You can find north in the street.
You can find north in the park.
You can find north in a boat.
All you have to do is to let this magnet
hang from the end of a string.
Wait until it stops turning.
The end that you marked with an N
will always point toward the north.

You can also use your magnet
to help you find the other directions — south,
east, and west. Do this:

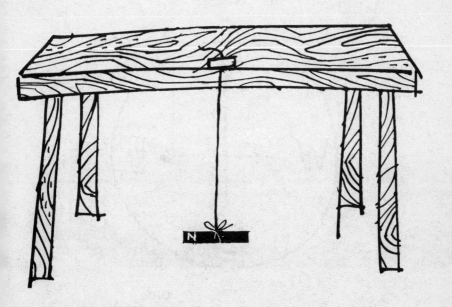

Fasten the other end of the string that is on
your magnet to a table top. Let the magnet
hang close to the floor.

Now draw a large circle on a sheet
of paper.

Write the letters of the four directions
this way on your paper:

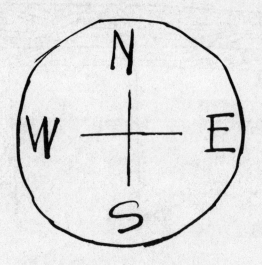

Place the paper on the floor under
the magnet.

You know that when the magnet
stops turning, one end will point toward
the north.

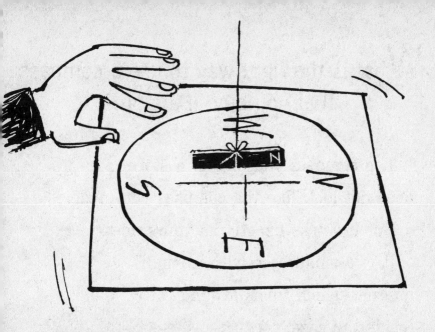

Turn the paper so that the letter N
is under the magnet end that points north.

You have made your own compass!

Now you can find the other directions —
south, east, and west.

Look at your paper.

The letter S shows you where south is.

The letter E shows you where east is.

The letter W shows you where west is.

You have read your own compass!

What is the right way to use a compass that you buy in a store?

The compass you buy in a store
does not look like the compass you made.

But it works exactly as yours does.

It is a small case with a small
magnet which turns around
inside the case.

The directions north, south, east, and west
are printed under the magnet.

This compass is used just as
yours was used to find directions.

Sometimes one end of the magnet is
darker than the other end.

The darker end of the magnet
always points north.

Turn the case around slowly.

Watch the letter N.

When it is under the end of the magnet

that points north, you have found north.

You can also find east, south, and west,
just as you did with your homemade compass.

You can use this compass to find
direction wherever you may be — in the house,
in the street, in the park, in a boat.

Keep the compass away from anything that has iron in it.

The magnet pointer in the compass would turn toward the iron. Then the compass would not work correctly.

Do you know who uses this kind of compass?

Boy Scouts

captains of ships

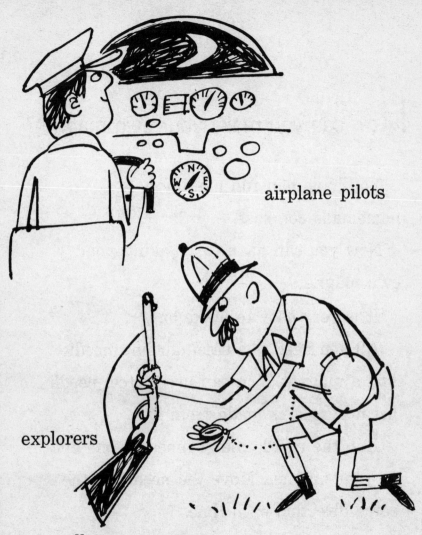

airplane pilots

explorers

— all use a compass.

Compasses help many people find direction
on the land, on the seas,
and in the air.

How can you make your own magnet?

You have had fun making a homemade compass.

Now you can have fun making your own magnet.

It is very easy to make one!

All you need is a steel darning needle and a magnet. You can use a steel needle because steel is made from iron.

Rub the needle many times on one end of your magnet. Move the needle in the same direction each time.

And then —

touch the needle to a paper clip.

The clip sticks to the needle!

You have made your own magnet!

This needle-magnet works the same

way as any other magnet.

You can use this needle-magnet to
pick up small things made of iron or steel.

You can use this magnet as
the magnet pointer of your homemade
compass.

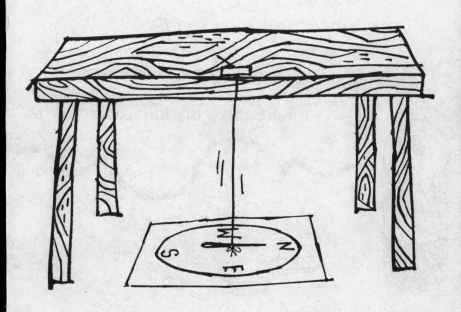

How can you make
an on-and-off magnet?

When you rubbed the darning needle
with your magnet, you made a magnet
that will work for a long time.

Would you like to know how to make
a magnet that works only when
you want it to work? You need

a long iron nail,

a long piece of thin, covered wire,

a few clips,

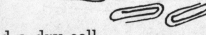

and a dry cell.

The dry cell is used to make electricity.

Wind the wire around the nail about
twenty times.

Take off the covering of both
ends of the wire.

Connect *one* bare end of the wire to *one*
screw on top of the dry cell.

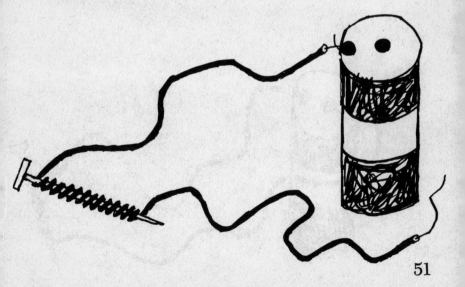

Try to pick up the clips with one end
of the nail.

Do not be unhappy if the nail does
not pick up the clips.

You have not yet made your on-and-off
magnet.

But —

connect the *other* end of the wire to
the *second* screw on the top of the dry cell.

Leave the first end of the wire
connected to the first screw.

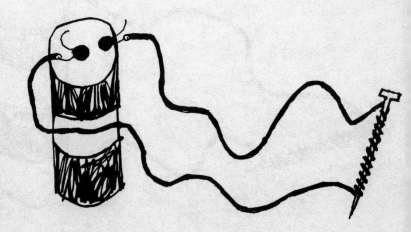

Now touch the nail to the clips.

Surprised?

The nail picks up the clips.

You have made a magnet!

What will happen to these clips
if you disconnect one end of the wire
from the dry cell?

Try it!

You will see that the clips will drop
to the table.

Why did the clips fall off the nail?

The nail has stopped being a magnet!

Put the wire back on the screw
and try to pick up the clips once more.

It works again!

The nail is a magnet again!

Take the wire off.

The clips fall off!

The nail is not a magnet!

Can you guess why these things
happen each time?

What goes on when both ends of the wire
are connected to the dry-cell screws?

Electricity from the dry cell
keeps going through the wire
that is wound around the nail.

This is what makes the nail become
a magnet.

As soon as the wire is disconnected,
the electricity stops going through the wire.

The nail stops being a magnet.

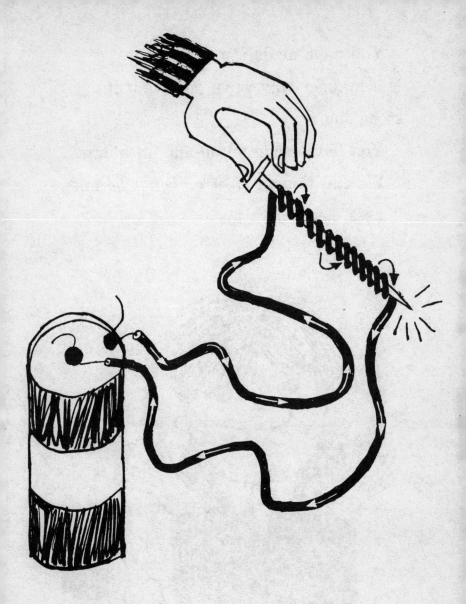

You have made a magnet that
is a magnet only when you want it
to be one.

You have made an on-and-off magnet.

We call this an *electromagnet* because
it uses electricity.

How can an electromagnet pick up and drop a heavy load?

People who work in scrap-iron yards use a very large electromagnet. This makes their work easier.

They make their electromagnet from a large iron plate instead of a nail.

They use *heavy* covered wire instead of thin covered wire.

They use a great deal of electricity instead of the little electricity of a dry cell.

When the workers are ready to pick up heavy pieces of iron, they move the plate onto the pieces. Then they turn on the electricity.

The electricity goes through the wire. The iron plate becomes a magnet!

And —

    it picks up the heavy iron pieces.

    When the workers are ready to put

the iron pieces into a truck,

this is what they do:

    They move the plate holding the

iron pieces over the truck.

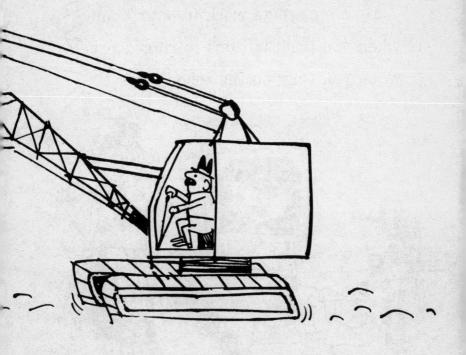

Then they turn off the electricity.

The electricity stops going through the wire.

The iron plate stops being a magnet.

The iron pieces drop into the truck.

They have made their electromagnet
work for them.

Where do electromagnets
work in your home?

Electromagnets work in your home

when you push buttons to ring doorbells,

when you turn on the television set,

when Mother uses the vacuum cleaner

or the washing machine,

— and when you run your electric train.

You do not see the electromagnets.

They are hidden in the bells,

in the machines, and in your engine.

But —

they are at work when the electricity

goes through the wires around the

electromagnets.

Electromagnets help to make work easier.

Long magnets
Short magnets
Fat magnets
Thin magnets
We use them in many ways.